THE HEART AND BLOOD

Revised Edition

Steve Parker

Series Consultant
Dr Alan Maryon-Davis
MB, BChir, MSc, MRCP, FFCM

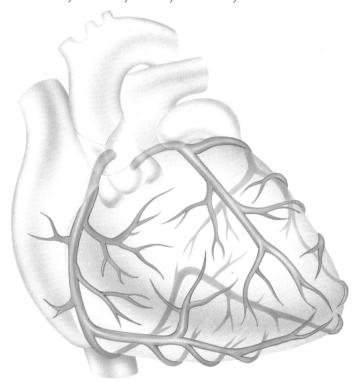

Franklin Watts
New York ● London ● Toronto ● Sydney

Words marked in bold appear in the glossary.

Original edition first published in 1982

First published in the United States by
Franklin Watts Inc.
387 Park Avenue South
New York 10016

Library of Congress Cataloging-in-Publication Data

Parker, Steve.
    The heart and blood.

    (Human body)
    Includes index.
    Summary: Discusses the heart, arteries, veins, blood, and other parts of the
body's circulatory system and the causes and prevention of coronary heart disease.
    1. Cardiovascular system – Physiology – Juvenile literature. 2. Coronary
heart disease – Juvenile literature. [1. Heart. 2. Blood. 3. Circulatory system]
I. Title. II. Series: Parker, Steve. Human body.
QP103.P37 1989   612.1   88-51610
ISBN 0-531-10711-6

Illustrations: Andrew Aloof, Bob Chapman, Howard Dyke,
Hayward Art Group, David Holmes, Abdul Aziz Khan, David
Mallot.

Photographs: Chris Fairclough 34, 41; Camilla Jessel 12; Science
Photo Library: front cover, 7, 14, 15, 17, 22, 24, 27, 28, 33, 39, 45t,
45b; John Watney 18; ZEFA 8.

Printed in Belgium

Contents

Introduction

Whether you are running a race, sitting quietly, or even sleeping, there is one part of your body that is always moving. It is a fist-sized organ, made mostly of muscle, in the middle of your chest. The muscle is divided into four hollow chambers that contain **blood**. More than once each second, every day, throughout life, the chambers contract with a rhythmic "lub-dup" noise. The muscle is the **heart**, and its regular contraction is the heartbeat.

The heart is a pump. As it contracts, it forces blood through a network of tubes called the blood vessels that spread through the whole body. The heart pumps the same blood around and around, which is why the heart and blood vessels are often called the **circulatory system.**

As it travels through the body, blood carries out many essential jobs. It carries life-giving **oxygen** and nutrients to the millions of cells, the tiny "building-blocks" of the body. It removes waste materials produced by the cells' life processes. Blood distributes special chemicals, called **hormones**, that coordinate the body's growth, development and internal activities. It also fights disease, spreads warmth evenly around the body, seals wounds and repairs injuries.

The blood must be kept moving, so that it can keep all the cells continuously supplied with their needs – especially oxygen. If the supply of oxygen fails for more than a few minutes, cells start to die. The heart keeps the blood flowing. If it stops, then within a few minutes the whole body dies.

Blood and the heart

- An average adult human contains about 5 liters (5.3 qt) of blood.
- The blood makes up about one-thirteenth of the body's weight.
- The adult heart weighs about 280 grams (10 oz).
- At rest, the heart pumps out about 70 milliliters (2.4 oz) of blood with each beat.
- The heart beats, on average, 70 times each minute at rest.
- This means all the blood is circulated (goes round the body once) in about one minute.
- During strenuous exercise, the heart can pump six to eight times the amount of blood that it pumps at rest.

4

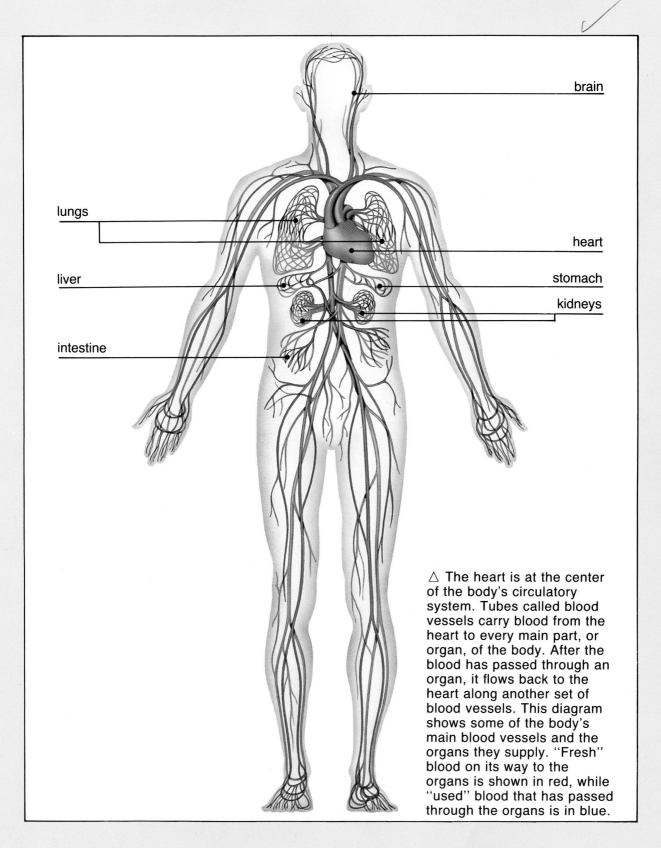

brain

lungs

heart

liver

stomach

kidneys

intestine

△ The heart is at the center of the body's circulatory system. Tubes called blood vessels carry blood from the heart to every main part, or organ, of the body. After the blood has passed through an organ, it flows back to the heart along another set of blood vessels. This diagram shows some of the body's main blood vessels and the organs they supply. "Fresh" blood on its way to the organs is shown in red, while "used" blood that has passed through the organs is in blue.

The blood vessels

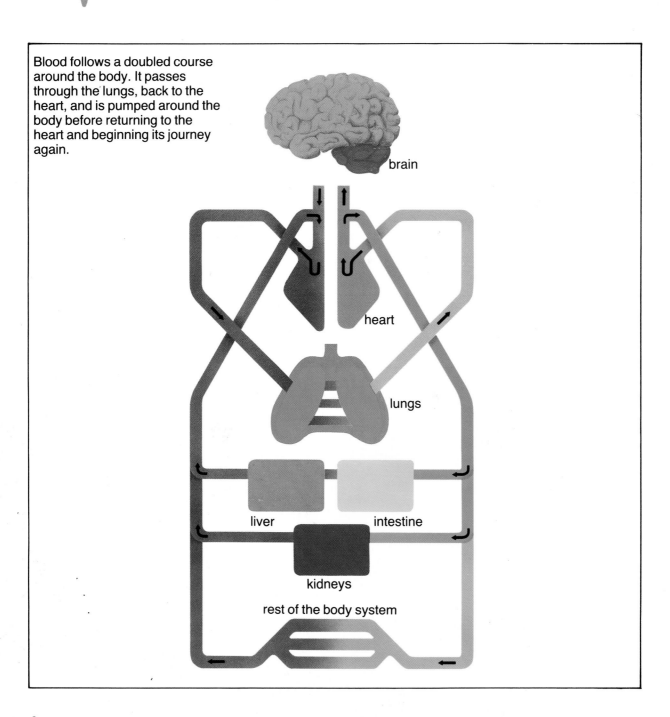

Blood follows a doubled course around the body. It passes through the lungs, back to the heart, and is pumped around the body before returning to the heart and beginning its journey again.

brain

heart

lungs

liver

intestine

kidneys

rest of the body system

There are three main kinds of blood vessels – **arteries**, **capillaries** and **veins**. Arteries are large vessels that carry blood away from the heart. Where an artery reaches an organ, it divides many times, becoming smaller and smaller until the tiny vessels can be seen only under a microscope. These are capillaries. Eventually the capillaries join together again to form a larger vessel called a vein, that returns blood to the heart.

In fact the heart is two pumps, side by side. Blood follows a "figure-8" course as it travels around the body. Starting in the right side of the heart, blood is pumped out along arteries to the lungs. In the lung capillaries it absorbs oxygen and becomes bright red. Then it flows back along veins to the left side of the heart. It is pumped out from the left side, along other arteries, to all the organs in the body. In the capillaries of each organ, blood gives up its oxygen to the cells and becomes a darker, reddish-blue color. Then it is carried back along veins to the right side of the heart.

▽ An artist's impression of blood cells flowing through a small blood vessel. The red doughnut-shaped cells are red blood cells **(erythrocytes)** which transport oxygen around the body. The small whitish blobs are platelets **(thrombocytes)**, which are involved in blood clotting and also help to repair damage to the lining of the vessel. The lining itself is made of flat endothelial cells joined together like curved paving slabs.

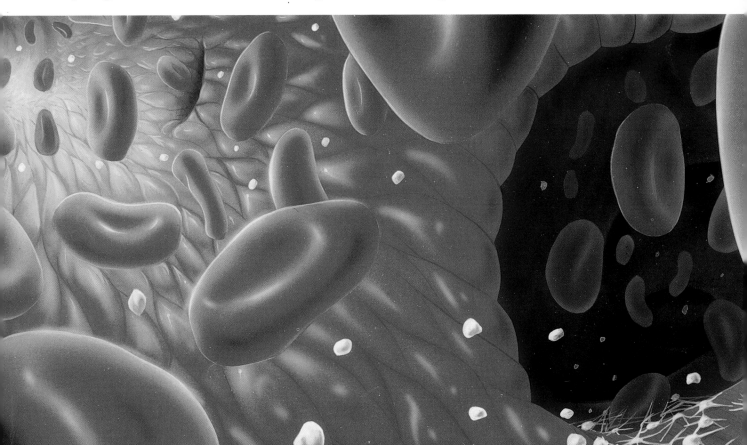

Structure of the heart

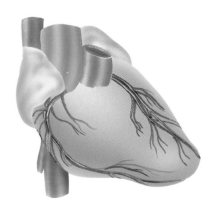

△ Front view of the human heart, showing the main vessels carrying blood to and from the muscular chambers.

The heart sits in the front of the chest, just behind the ribs. It is wrapped in a thin, slippery "skin," the **pericardium**, which lubricates its beating movements. About two-thirds of the heart is on the left of the body's midline.

More than half of the heart's weight is muscle. It is a specialized type of muscle called **cardiac muscle** or myocardium. Many muscles in the body, such as those which move the arms and legs, become tired or "fatigued" after much use, and they can no longer work. Cardiac muscle never fatigues.

A network of tough fibers is embedded in the heart muscle. This gives the heart a certain amount

▷ Echocardiography produces a "sound picture" of the heart, in the same way that an ultrasound scan shows a baby in the womb. Extremely high-pitched sound waves (ultrasound) are beamed into the chest by the hand-held emitter. A sensor in the emitter casing detects the echoes from organs in the chest, which are then processed by a computer and shown on the screen. The procedure is painless and the display shows "live" pictures of the beating heart.

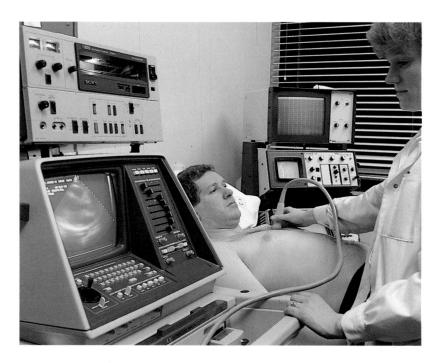

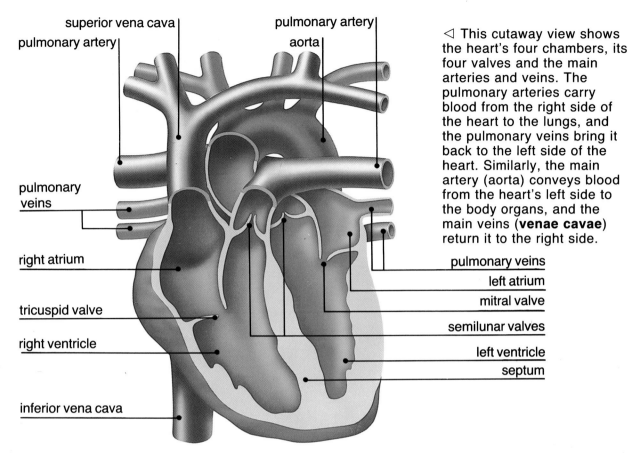

superior vena cava

pulmonary artery

pulmonary artery

aorta

pulmonary veins

right atrium

tricuspid valve

right ventricle

inferior vena cava

pulmonary veins

left atrium

mitral valve

semilunar valves

left ventricle

septum

◁ This cutaway view shows the heart's four chambers, its four valves and the main arteries and veins. The pulmonary arteries carry blood from the right side of the heart to the lungs, and the pulmonary veins bring it back to the left side of the heart. Similarly, the main artery (aorta) conveys blood from the heart's left side to the body organs, and the main veins (**venae cavae**) return it to the right side.

of rigidity, yet allows it to change shape as it contracts to squeeze out blood.

Each side of the heart is divided into two chambers. The upper chamber is the **atrium**. It has a thin wall and receives blood coming back to the heart along veins. At the base of the atrium is a one-way valve that allows blood to move from the upper to the lower chamber, but not the other way. This helps to insure that blood travels one way around the system, rather than flowing to and fro with each heartbeat.

The lower chamber, the **ventricle**, has a thick, muscular wall. This contracts with great force to push blood out of the heart into the arteries. At the exit from the ventricle there is another valve, the semilunar valve, which again makes sure blood travels in the correct direction around the body.

▽ The junction of the heart and **aorta** has been sliced open and flattened to show the three pocket-like cusps of the aortic valve. Normally the flexible cusps butt together to make a "bloodproof" seal.

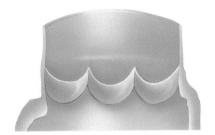

The heart as a pump

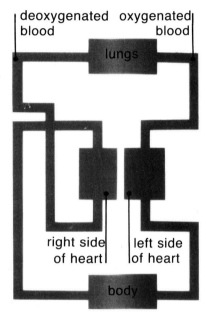

deoxygenated blood   oxygenated blood

lungs

right side of heart   left side of heart

body

△ The body's "double circulation," with the heart at the center.

It is very important that "fresh," bright red blood circulate directly to the body's organs without mixing with the "used" dark reddish-blue blood. This is partly because the oxygen (O_2) in fresh blood must be delivered to the organs as quickly as possible, without being mixed and diluted by used blood.

Also, used blood contains a lot of **carbon dioxide** (CO_2). This is a waste material produced by the activities of the cells, and picked up by the blood as it flows through the capillaries in each organ. The used blood must be sent to the lungs, by way of the heart, where the carbon dioxide is removed and breathed out. This means that there is an "exchange of gases" in the lungs; oxygen is absorbed from the air into the blood, while carbon dioxide passes from the blood to the air. Breathing

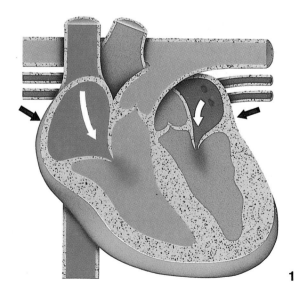

1

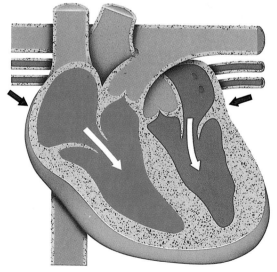

2

brings in extra oxygen from the outside air, and gets rid of carbon dioxide from the lungs.

This is why the heart has two sides, separated by a sheet of muscle called the **septum**. There are, in effect, two circulations. The right side of the heart sends used, carbon dioxide-rich blood to the lungs. This is called the pulmonary circulation. The left side deals with fresh, oxygen-rich blood and sends it to the other body organs. This is the systemic circulation.

During each heartbeat, the various chambers contract at slightly different times. But they do so in a coordinated manner, so that blood flows smoothly from one part of the heart to the next (page 14). The "lub-dup" sound of a heartbeat is the noise of the valves snapping shut after blood has flowed through them.

▽ The four stages of a heartbeat, which all occur in less than one second.
1 Fresh, oxygen-rich blood (red) enters the left atrium, and used blood (blue) flows into the right atrium.
2 Blood passes from the atria through valves into the ventricles. The semilunar valves at the exits to the ventricles close, so that blood is not pushed in from the arteries.
3 The ventricles begin to contract, closing the atrial valves and stopping blood from leaking back into the atria.
4 The ventricles contract fully, and blood pushes open the semilunar valves and is squirted out into the main arteries.

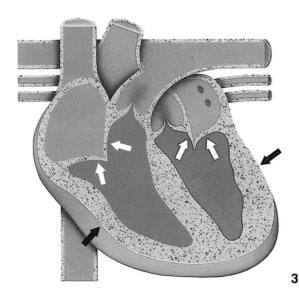

3

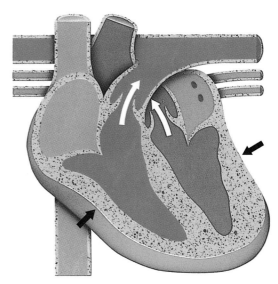

4.

The beating heart

△ Busy writing, this boy hardly notices having his wrist pulse checked by the nurse. She looks at her watch and counts the number of heartbeats in a certain time. The boy's body temperature is also being taken by the thermometer in his mouth. Simple checks like these can give early warning of disease, as well as showing how well people are recovering from illness.

During a heartbeat, each contraction of the ventricle sends a powerful jet of blood surging into the arteries. Then, as the ventricle relaxes and refills before the next beat, the blood flow slows down. These "surges" of blood cause the flexible walls of the arteries to bulge outward slightly. The bulges, or pressure waves, from successive heartbeats travel along each artery like ripples from a stone thrown into a pool.

These pressure waves ripple along all the main arteries, but it is convenient to feel for them in the few places where an artery runs near the surface of the body, just below the skin. Such places include one side of the neck, behind the knee and in the wrist. We call the pulsations of the artery the "pulse." In the wrist, each pulse corresponds to a pressure wave that starts with the contraction of the left ventricle and travels along the artery, through the chest and shoulder and down the arm to the wrist.

The number of pulses in one minute is known as the pulse rate. This is the same as the number of heartbeats in one minute (the heart rate). The average pulse rate at rest is about 70. In a new baby the normal rate is around 120, but this gradually decreases with age.

During strenuous exercise, the pulse rate may increase to over 150. This is because the body's muscles are working hard and they need more oxygen than they do at rest, so the heart has to pump faster to keep up with their demands.

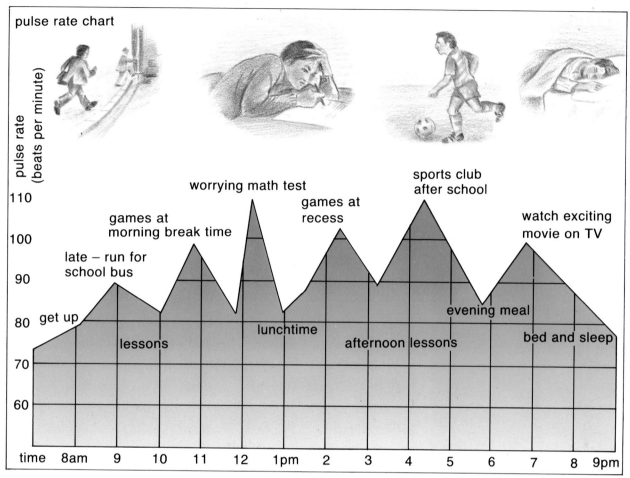

pulse rate chart

pulse rate (beats per minute)

late – run for school bus

games at morning break time

worrying math test

games at recess

sports club after school

watch exciting movie on TV

get up

lessons

lunchtime

afternoon lessons

evening meal

bed and sleep

110
100
90
80
70
60

time 8am   9   10   11   12   1pm   2   3   4   5   6   7   8 9pm

Pulse rate can help to give an idea of a person's general fitness. The right kinds of exercise make the heart pump harder and faster, to supply the working muscles with the extra blood they need. Since the heart itself is made of muscle, it becomes stronger and fitter with exercise. The heart of an inactive person tends to beat faster than average at rest, and it pumps out less blood at each beat. With a suitable training program, the resting pulse rate should gradually become slower, and also the heart should recover more quickly after exercise. The heart of a very fit person often beats at a slower-than-average rate at rest. Some top sports players have resting pulse rates of 60, or even 50, compared to the average of around 70.

△ This imaginary chart shows how a child's pulse (heart) rate might vary during an average day. When the body is relaxed and not very active, such as during lessons, the rate is slower. During activity and excitement, such as playing sports or watching an adventure movie, the heart speeds up and pumps faster.

13

The pacemaker

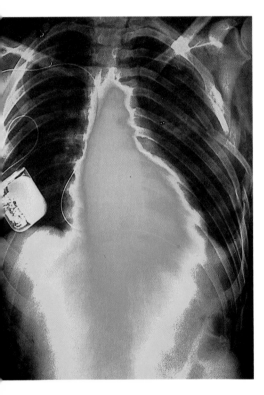

△ This X-ray of an artificial pacemaker inside a person's chest has been colored by computer to make it clearer. The pacemaker is on the left, its battery and internal circuits visible under the X-rays. A long loop of wire connects it to the heart, which is the blue region in the middle.

Most muscles in the body are controlled by small bursts of electricity called nerve signals. A nerve signal travels from the brain along a nerve to the muscle, where it causes the tiny fibers that make up the muscle to shorten, or contract. The heart is mostly muscle, but it has its own self-contained timing mechanism that makes it beat at a steady rate. This is called the **pacemaker**. The rate of beating, and the strength of each beat, are altered by nerve signals from the brain and by hormones, which are special chemicals in the blood.

The pacemaker, also called the sino-atrial (SA) node, is a small patch of cells in the rear wall of the right atrium. The cells generate electrical signals, similar to the signals that travel along nerves. About once each second, the pacemaker cells send out a burst of these electrical signals, which spread through the heart muscle, around the wall of the right atrium and across to the left atrium. On the way, the signals cause the tiny cardiac muscle fibers to shorten. This makes the whole chamber contract, from the top downward, squeezing blood from each atrium down into its ventricle.

If the electrical signals continued to spread down through the ventricles, they would cause these chambers to contract from the top downward. But this would trap blood in the bases of the ventricles, rather than pushing it upward, out into the arteries. Preventing this is the job of a second patch of specialized cells, the atrio-ventricular (AV) node. This is located where the atria join the ventricles, almost at the very center of the heart.

The AV node acts as a relay station. It detects each burst of signals from the pacemaker and sends it on, down a specialized nerve-like pathway through the ventricular wall, to the bases of the ventricles. Here the signals spread out and travel up through the ventricular wall, causing a wave of contraction in the correct direction, from the base upward.

The signals that trigger and coordinate each heartbeat do not stay in the heart. The body is a good conductor of electricity, and electrical "echoes" spread out from the heart, through the organs to the skin. In a machine called an electrocardiograph, sensitive electrodes (electrical detectors) attached to the skin pick up the signals and display them on a paper chart or television screen. The display is an **electrocardiogram**, or ECG, a recording of the heart's electrical activity.

▽ Emergency treatment for a heartattack victim. In the foreground, the nurse holds the two large electrodes of a cardiac defibrillator on the patient's chest. A burst of electricity is fed between the electrodes, through the heart, with the aim of "shocking" it back into a regular beat. The face mask supplies oxygen, to enable as much oxygen as possible to enter the blood.

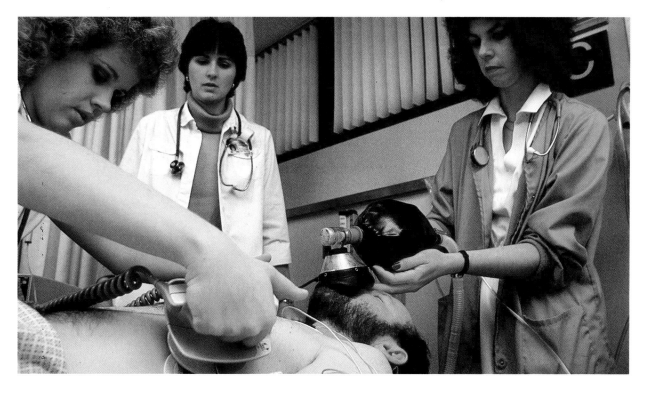

The arteries

Arteries are the tubes that carry blood away from the heart. They are elastic, thick-walled vessels, able to withstand the surge of blood from each heartbeat as the ventricles contract.

The left ventricle squeezes blood into the aorta, the largest artery in the body. The aorta is about three centimeters (1 in) in diameter and arches upward, then to the left and downward, looping behind the heart to go down into the abdomen. As the left ventricle contracts, blood surges into the aorta under great pressure, traveling at a speed of about 40 centimeters (16 in) per second. Along its length, the aorta branches to form many smaller

▽ **1** Each heartbeat pushes a jet of blood through the left semilunar valve into the aorta, the main artery. The pressure of the jet causes the artery wall to expand.
2 As the pressure wave moves along the artery, the wall behind it recoils to give the blood inside a secondary "push" on its way. The recoil also closes the semilunar valve, preventing backflow of blood into the heart.

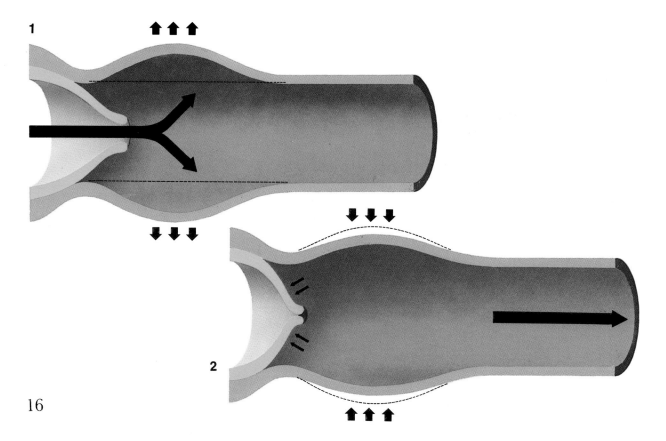

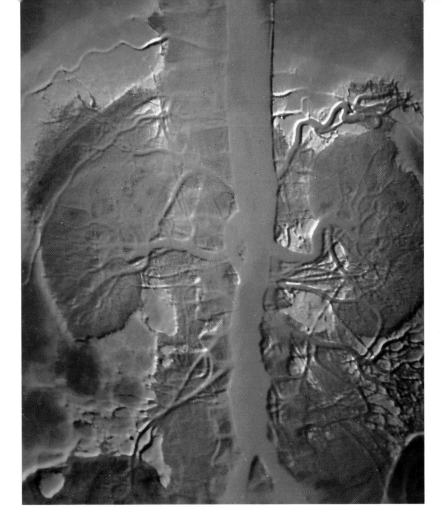

◁ The main arteries inside the middle of the body are shown by arteriography (angiography). Special dye, which shows up on an X-ray, is injected into the blood vessels, and a computer colors the resulting picture for easy viewing. Here the main aorta (reddish-pink) passes down the middle of the picture, and arteries branch off into the two kidneys on either side. The bones of the spine (red) show up behind.

arteries that take blood to the individual organs. The pressure and speed of the blood falls as the arteries continue to branch and become smaller.

The wall of an artery has several layers. On the inside is the endothelium, a smooth and "bloodproof" lining that keeps blood from leaking out. On the outside is a tough, fibrous covering which is elastic and has a certain amount of "give." Sandwiched between these is a layer of muscle.

The artery wall bulges with each heartbeat. Then, because it is elastic, the wall "recoils" as the pressure wave travels onward. The recoil continues to squeeze blood on its way, even as the heart relaxes between contractions. In this way the pressurized, jerky spurts of blood are gradually smoothed out, so that they do not damage the delicate capillaries farther on.

The blood vessels of the heart

Heart disease

- Gradual narrowing of the coronary arteries starves the heart muscle of nourishment and oxygen.
- If the blockage is minor or temporary, the heart gets a "cramp" and this causes the chest pain called **angina**. If the sufferer rests, the pain passes.
- If the blockage is more serious, the heart stops working and starts to die.
- Heart attacks are a major cause of death in Western countries.

Every organ in the body needs a blood supply, and the heart is no exception. For several reasons, although the heart is full of blood, it cannot use this blood to nourish its own muscle. When the heart contracts, blood in its chambers is at such great pressure that it would tear any small vessels leading directly into its walls. Also, the blood in the right side of the heart is very low in oxygen (because it is on its way to the lungs), so the muscular walls on that side would not receive enough oxygen if they were supplied with blood from inside the heart.

So the heart, like any other organ, has its own blood vessels. These are the coronary arteries and veins. The two coronary arteries branch from the beginning of the main aorta, just after it has left the heart. These soon divide to form a network of small arteries across the surface of the heart. (The name "coronary" comes from the Latin word *coronarius*,

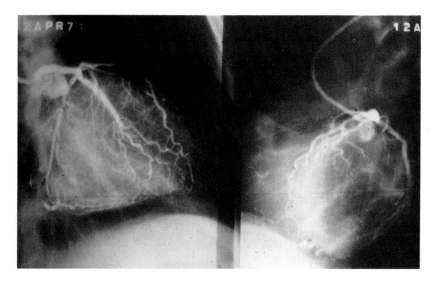

▷ In coronary arteriography, a dye that shows up on X-rays is injected into the coronary arteries. The branching pattern of the arteries is then clearly seen "live" on the X-ray screen. This technique can locate narrowings of the coronary arteries which may cause a heart attack.

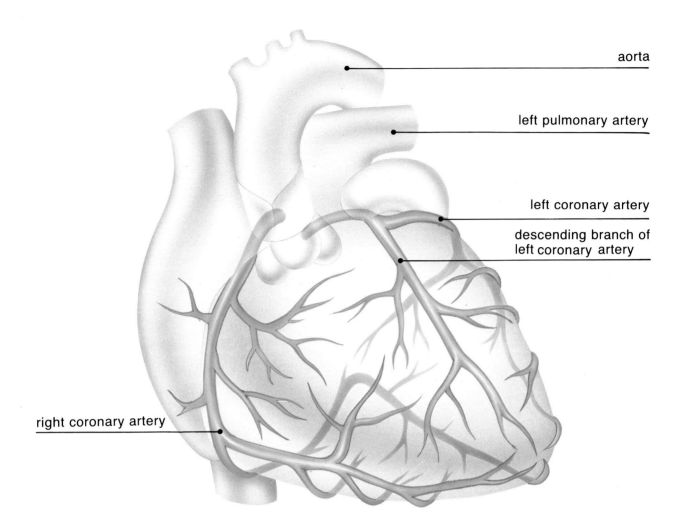

aorta

left pulmonary artery

left coronary artery

descending branch of
left coronary artery

right coronary artery

which means "belonging to a wreath or crown,"
since these arteries encircle the top of the heart like
a crown on the head.)

The coronary arteries eventually enter the heart
muscle and divide still further, into capillaries that
carry oxygen and nourishment to every muscle
fiber. The capillaries join to form coronary veins.

The coronary arteries are vital, although they are
only the size of drinking straws. If they become
diseased or blocked for some reason, they prevent
fresh blood reaching the heart muscle, and so the
heart cannot pump effectively.

△ The coronary arteries trace
a branching path across the
heart's surface, before turning
inward to supply the heart
muscle itself with blood.

19

The veins

At any moment, almost three-quarters of the body's blood is in the veins. The veins are thin-walled, stretchy tubes that transport blood from the lungs and other organs back to the heart.

The walls of veins contain the same layers that are found in the arteries, but the layers are much thinner. By the time blood has passed along the arteries and through the capillary network of each organ, it has lost its surges of pressure. Since the veins do not have to cope with the same strains as the arteries, their walls can be thin and pliable.

The largest veins can change their capacity by

1 Blood flowing the correct way through a vein pushes open the tough, rubbery valve flaps.
2 If blood tries to travel the wrong way, the valves close. Sometimes, especially in the legs, the valves do not work effectively and the veins become swollen and painful. These **"varicose veins"** can sometimes be seen just under the skin.

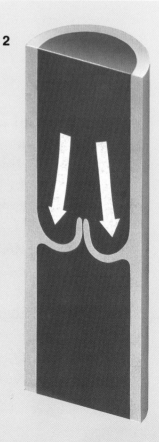

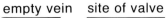

massage blood upward   empty vein   site of valve   vein refills

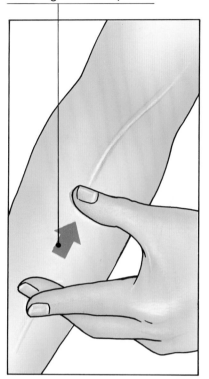

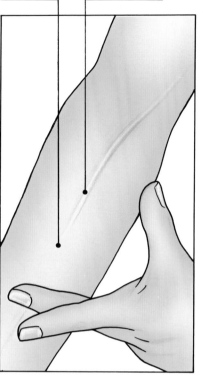

slowly contracting the muscles in their walls. This makes up for any changes in blood volume that may occur after serious bleeding.

Most of the larger veins contain one-way valves, like the valves in the heart. These ensure that blood will not collect in a vein, but continue to flow slowly back to the heart. In people who stand still for long periods, blood tends to collect in the ankles and legs, since the heart's pumping pressure is not strong enough to overcome gravity and force the blood back up on the long journey from the feet. When walking, the leg muscles squeeze the veins and help to push blood back up to the heart. Soldiers standing at attention or at parade rest are taught to tense their leg muscles periodically to help the blood circulate. If they forget, blood collecting in the lower body can cause a shortage of blood to the brain, causing fainting.

△ Demonstrate the valves in your own veins by this simple experiment. Press two fingers over the main vein on the inside of your forearm, about halfway between elbow and wrist, to temporarily stop the blood flowing up it. Massage the blood in the vein upward with your thumb (above left). Take your thumb away, and blood should not leak back down past the valve (above middle). Take your fingers away and the vein refills from below as blood once again flows up your arm (above right).

The smallest blood vessels

▽ Red blood cells line up to pass through a capillary, in this scanning electron microscope photograph.

If all the blood vessels in the body were joined end to end in a single line, they would stretch an amazing 93,000 miles – almost halfway to the Moon! Most of the length would be made up of capillaries, the body's smallest blood vessels, which are visible only under a microscope. Yet these vessels hold only one-twentieth of the body's blood.

The capillary network is so dense that few cells in the body are far from one of these blood vessels. The wall of a capillary is only one cell thick, and made of very thin, curved cells named endothelial cells, joined together like a tube-shaped jigsaw puzzle. The cells are "leaky," and they allow oxygen, nutrients and other substances to pass from the fresh blood inside the capillary to the cells outside. Also, carbon dioxide and other waste products can pass from the surrounding cells through the capillary wall into the blood, to be taken away for disposal.

The capillary walls allow not only dissolved substances to pass through. Complete cells, particularly the white blood cells of the body's defense system, can flatten themselves and "ooze" through the joins between the cells of the capillary wall (page 28). In this way, white cells can pass from the blood into surrounding tissues, to fight disease there. They can also return from the tissues into the bloodstream, to be carried quickly to another site in the body where they are required.

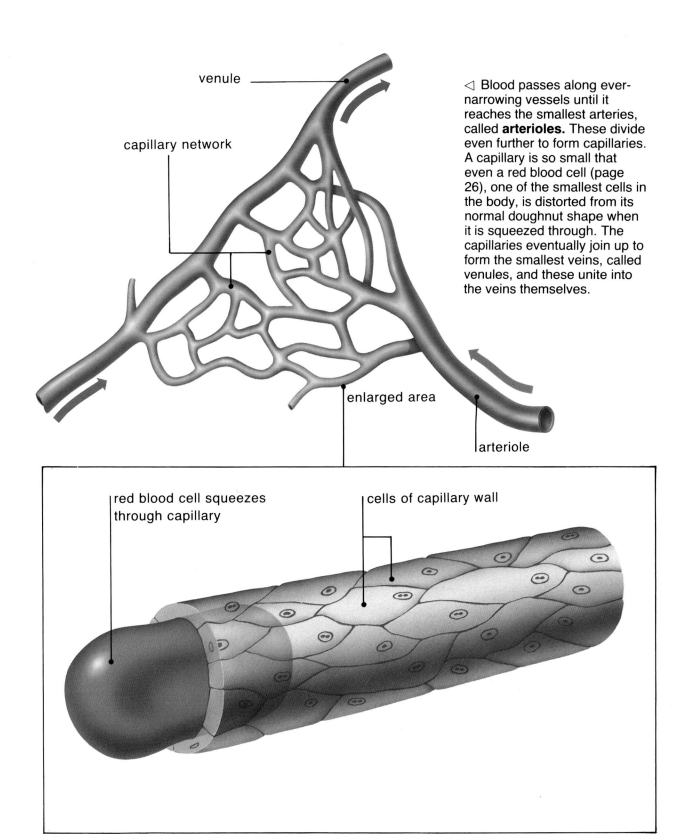

venule

capillary network

enlarged area

arteriole

◁ Blood passes along ever-narrowing vessels until it reaches the smallest arteries, called **arterioles.** These divide even further to form capillaries. A capillary is so small that even a red blood cell (page 26), one of the smallest cells in the body, is distorted from its normal doughnut shape when it is squeezed through. The capillaries eventually join up to form the smallest veins, called venules, and these unite into the veins themselves.

red blood cell squeezes through capillary

cells of capillary wall

Measuring blood pressure

Great force is needed to push blood around the system, through the tiny blood vessels. The force is provided by the constantly beating heart, and this means that blood in the circulatory system is always being pushed hard, to make it flow. In other words, the blood is under pressure.

In fact, the blood pressure is always changing. It rises to a peak as the ventricle contracts to force a surge of blood out of the heart. Then it falls slightly as the ventricle relaxes and refills with blood. The recoil of the artery walls keeps the blood flowing between contractions. Also, the farther blood travels from the left side of the heart, the lower its pressure. It is at its highest in the left ventricle and aorta, lower in the small arteries leading away from

▽ Measuring blood pressure is a quick and painless procedure. It can give early warning of possible problems in various parts of the body, such as the eyes and kidneys, as well as disease in the heart and blood vessels.

the heart, lower still in the capillaries, and almost non-existent in the large veins that return blood to the right side of the heart.

Doctors always measure blood pressure at the same place in the body. Then they can compare readings from the same person over time, and compare readings between different people. The standard place to measure blood pressure is in the artery of the upper arm. The doctor or nurse uses a device called a **sphygmomanometer** and takes two pressure readings.

The first measures the peak pressure at systole (pronounced "sis'-toll-ee"), when the heart contracts with the greatest force and the pressure bulge travels down the artery of the arm. This reading is the systolic blood pressure.

The second measurement is the lowest pressure, at diastole ("die-ass'-toll-ee"), when the heart relaxes between contractions. This is called the diastolic pressure. The two numbers are written together, for example, 120/80. This is the blood pressure of a healthy young adult.

Blood pressure also varies according to activity. Someone who runs a race or who is very worried usually has a higher blood pressure than if he or she were relaxed and resting. If the resting blood pressure rises too high for any length of time, there is a risk of damage to delicate organs such as the brain, eyes and kidneys. Higher-than-normal blood pressure is called **hypertension**. Many people are advised to have their blood pressure checked every few years to make sure they do not have hypertension. This is particularly important as they get older. If they do have hypertension, they may be able to lose excess weight, exercise more, and perhaps take special medicines, to bring the pressure back to normal.

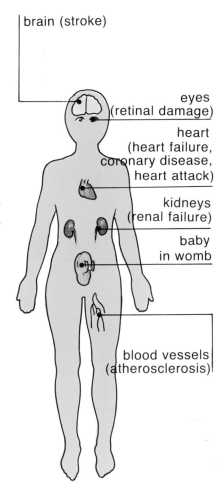

brain (stroke)

eyes (retinal damage)

heart (heart failure, coronary disease, heart attack)

kidneys (renal failure)

baby in womb

blood vessels (atherosclerosis)

△ Various parts of the body may be damaged if blood pressure stays unusually high for too long.

Oxygen carriers

Blood is a complicated substance. Just over half its volume is **plasma** (page 30), a yellowish liquid that contains body chemicals such as nutrients, hormones and minerals, floating in solution. The rest of its volume consists of various cells. The main types are red cells and white cells.

Red cells, or erythrocytes, are the body's oxygen carriers. They are extremely small, even for cells, and incredibly numerous. A typical red cell is only 0.007 millimeters (0.00028 in) across. And in one cubic milliliter (0.06 in^3) of blood (not much bigger than a pinhead) there are five million red cells.

Each red cell is shaped like a plump disk, hollowed slightly on each side. It contains some 270 million molecules of a special substance called **hemoglobin**, which has a great attraction for oxygen. In the lungs, oxygen from the air attaches itself to hemoglobin in the red cells. In doing so it

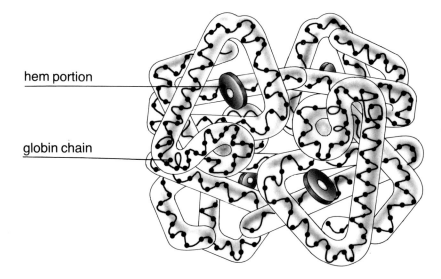

hem portion

globin chain

◁ This is a diagram of a molecule of hemoglobin, the oxygen-carrying substance found in blood cells. It is made of four long, folded chains of "globin" **protein** and four iron-containing "hem" portions, which are shown here as disks. Oxygen attaches to the hem portions.

forms **oxyhemoglobin**, which is bright red. This is why fresh, oxygen-rich blood is itself bright red.

Oxygen travels in the blood, joined to hemoglobin, until it reaches the capillaries. Here it passes through the capillary walls to the cells beyond. Hemoglobin that has given up its attached oxygen is referred to as **deoxyhemoglobin.** It is dark red – the color of used blood.

Old red cells become misshapen and unable to carry oxygen. They are broken down in the liver, spleen and bone marrow, and some of their contents are recycled to make new red cells.

Hemoglobin contains iron, and the body needs a certain amount of iron to keep up its production of red cells. If there is not enough iron in the diet, or if the red cells are faulty in some other way, the result is anemia. If you are anemic, you become pale and breathless, and tire easily.

△ This scanning electron microscope photograph shows five blood cells, about 6,000 times actual size. There are two normal, doughnut-shaped red blood cells, lower center and above right. The "spiky" cell is a special blood cell, an echinocyte. The two long, thin cells are sickled red blood cells, produced in the disorder called sickle cell anemia. They are deformed, stick in small capillaries, and they cannot carry oxygen efficiently.

White blood cells

White cells, or **leucocytes**, are the second main type of blood cell. Although they appear whitish under the microscope they are not truly white in color, but made of a fairly clear jelly-like substance. White cells are larger than red cells, and less numerous. There are about 10,000 in one cubic milliliter (0.06 in^3) of blood. White cells help to fight disease (pages 34 and 41).

White cells come in various shapes and sizes, and each kind does a different job. Three kinds have a grainy texture and because of this they are all called granulocytes. Individually they are called basophils, eosinophils and neutrophils. These names are derived from the special chemical stains used to color them in the microscope laboratory. The other two kinds of white cells are clear, not grainy. These are the **lymphocytes** and monocytes.

▽ Two macrophages (types of white blood cell) patrol the lungs in search of dust particles and invading germs. The lower one is spreading around a spherical foreign body to the left, ready to engulf and neutralize it.

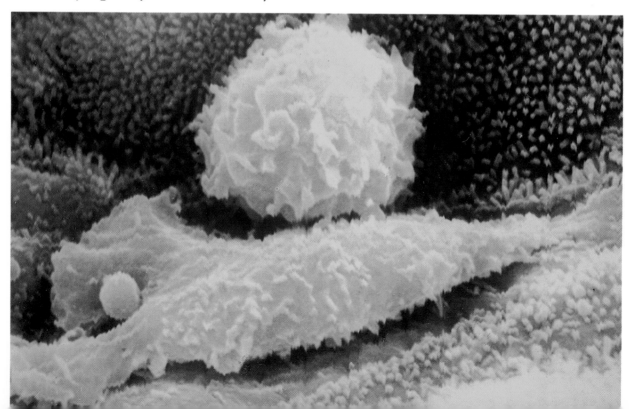

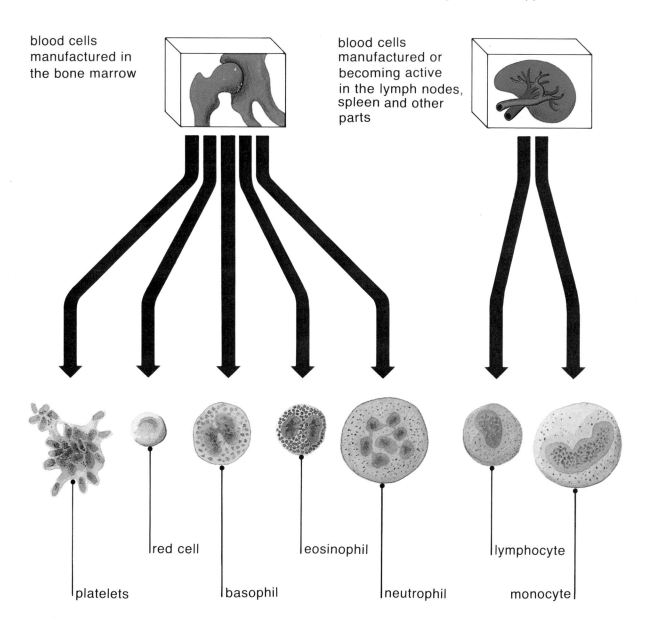

▽ Many blood cells, including red cells and some white cells, are made in the bone marrow. Some kinds of white cells are produced in other parts of the body, such as the **spleen**, **lymph nodes** and the thymus gland in the upper chest.

blood cells manufactured in the bone marrow

blood cells manufactured or becoming active in the lymph nodes, spleen and other parts

platelets

red cell

basophil

eosinophil

neutrophil

lymphocyte

monocyte

Plasma and platelets

Plasma is the straw-colored liquid part of blood that remains after the cells have been removed. It is more than nine-tenths water but contains an enormous range of dissolved chemicals. Proteins in the plasma are used to build and repair cells. Glucose, a type of sugar which is the body's main energy source, forms about one- to two-thousandths of the plasma. Other substances include minerals such as sodium, calcium and potassium, and waste materials such as carbon dioxide.

Red cells are not the smallest particles in the blood. Even smaller are **platelets**, or thrombocytes. A platelet is less than one-quarter the size of a red cell, and there are up to 500,000 (half a million) platelets in one cubic milliliter of blood. However, a platelet is not a true cell. It is more of a cell fragment, "nipped off" from a parent cell in the bone marrow, and it has an average life of less than two weeks.

Platelets help the blood to clot after an injury. They take part in a complicated series of more than a dozen chemical reactions that happen at the site of the injury. Damaged cells release substances that react with certain chemicals in the plasma, called clotting factors. A dissolved protein in the plasma, fibrinogen, is quickly converted into its insoluble form, **fibrin**. The long, yellow threads of fibrin make a tangled network that traps platelets and blood cells. Gradually a blood **clot** forms. This seals the injury, so that blood does not leak away, and healing can begin.

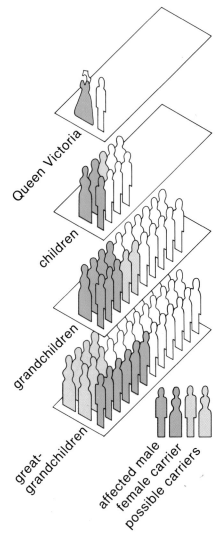

△ Hemophilia is a "bleeding disorder" in which blood fails to clot, owing to a lack of the clotting factor known as Factor VIII. It runs in families, including that of Queen Victoria, but affects only males.

30

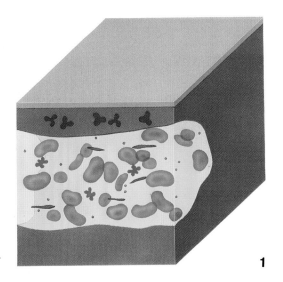

1

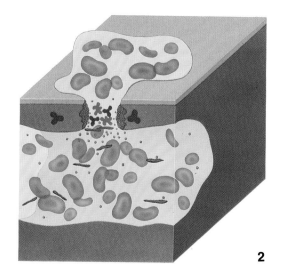

2

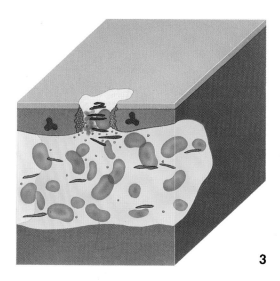

3

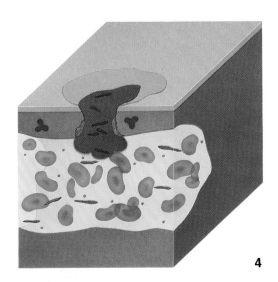

4

△ The clotting process relies on a series of chemical reactions involving various substances in the blood.
1 Blood flows smoothly through a healthy vessel.
2 The vessel is damaged, and blood begins to leak out. Various blood cells and chemicals begin to collect at the site.

3 Platelets react with chemicals to convert the fibrinogen in the plasma into long, sticky threads of fibrin. These form a mesh that traps blood cells, platelets and other debris to seal the break.
4 After a short time the fibrin threads shorten, squeezing the whole mass into a firm

lump. This is a blood clot, or **thrombus**, which seals the wound while the vessel wall is repaired. If the damage is a cut on the skin, the clot hardens in air to form a tough, protective scab.

Blood types

For many centuries, doctors tried to help those who had lost blood through injury, or who had a blood disease, by giving them blood from a healthy person, or donor. Unfortunately, this process was often no help at all – sometimes it caused the death of the recipient, instead of being a cure. The reason was discovered in the 1900s, by Austrian physician Karl Landsteiner.

Not all blood is the same. There are four main types, or groups, of blood. These are called A, B, AB and O. The differences have to do with special chemicals called agglutinogens on the "skin" of the red cells, and other chemicals termed agglutinins in the plasma. If blood from certain groups is mixed these chemicals cause the red cells to clump together, or agglutinate, and clog up the capillaries – with serious consequences.

▽ Blood groups are determined by the genes you inherit from your parents. Your group may not be the same as that of your parents, but only certain combinations of groups are possible. In the diagram, the first letter shows the person's actual blood group. The second letter is the blood group carried in the genes, which may show up in the children.

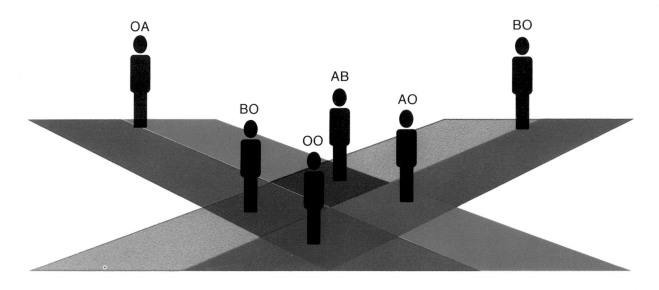

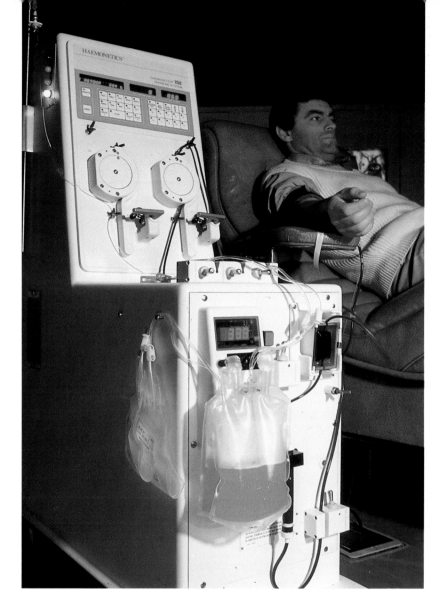

◁ Giving blood takes only a short time, and may well save someone's life. This man is giving plasma only (plasmapheresis). Some blood is withdrawn through a needle into a container, and the blood cells are allowed to settle to the bottom. The plasma portion of the blood is drawn off the top for storage, while the blood cells are returned to the donor's body.

It is usually safe to receive blood of your own group in the ABO system. Group O blood can be given to a recipient of any group, while an AB recipient can accept any group of blood.

But the ABO system is only one of many systems of **blood groups**. Another is the **Rhesus system**. Therefore, in practice, small samples of blood are tested to ensure they match before a **transfusion** is carried out. It is helpful to carry a card saying to which blood group you belong. Then, in an emergency, the medical team can save time by giving you the right kind of blood without having to test your blood group first.

White cells and antibodies

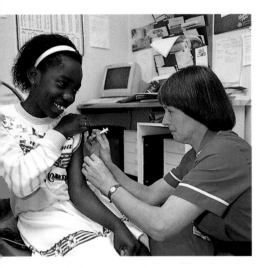

△ Immunization gives protection against possibly dangerous infections like measles, rubella (german measles), tetanus, polio, diphtheria and whooping cough. It takes only a few seconds and is not as painful as some people think!

Infections are caused by microscopic organisms such as bacteria and viruses, often called "germs." They enter the body through cuts and grazes, or through the delicate linings of the nose, throat, lungs or intestines. Once inside, they multiply and begin to damage the body's tissues. This produces the symptoms of the infection, such as fever and sore throat.

The white cells are the body's main defense against invading germs. Neutrophils, eosinophils and monocytes can "eat" germs by a process called phagocytosis. Basophils and certain lymphocytes release chemicals that begin the disease-fighting process of inflammation. The blood vessels widen, and white cells and germ-fighting substances of many kinds gather to do battle with the invaders.

Each type of germ has a characteristic pattern of chemicals, known as **antigens**, on its "skin." Certain lymphocytes recognize these chemicals and manufacture substances called **antibodies**. The antibodies attach to the germs and either kill them by breaking them apart, or make them clump together so that they can be devoured by white cells. Gradually the white cells overcome the germs, and the infection is brought under control.

After the infection has passed, some lymphocytes "remember" how to make the antibodies against those particular germs. In the future, when that type of germ enters the body again, the white cells can fight back at once, before the germ begins to multiply. This means the illness is stopped before it develops. The person is said to be **immune** to that particular infection.

It is possible to "infect" the body with killed or disabled germs. These cannot cause illness, but they do alert the defense system and make the body immune. This process is called immunization. In some cases the germs have to be injected into the body, while in others they can be taken by mouth. In many countries, babies and children receive a standard set of immunizations that protect them against serious infections such as diphtheria, tetanus, polio and whooping cough.

The germs for some infections, like the common cold and influenza ('flu), are always changing their "skins." This means that the white cells do not recognize them when they next appear, and as a result it is usually not possible to immunize the body against such infections.

▽ Some white cells "eat" germs whole, by the process of phagocytosis.
1 The white cell moves toward a string of germs, flowing like jelly.
2 Long "arms" flow out from the white cell and surround the germs.
3 The arms merge to trap the germs inside the white cell's body. Digestive chemicals attack the germs and break them into pieces.
4 Some white cells can then flow away, leaving behind the undigested remains of the germs.

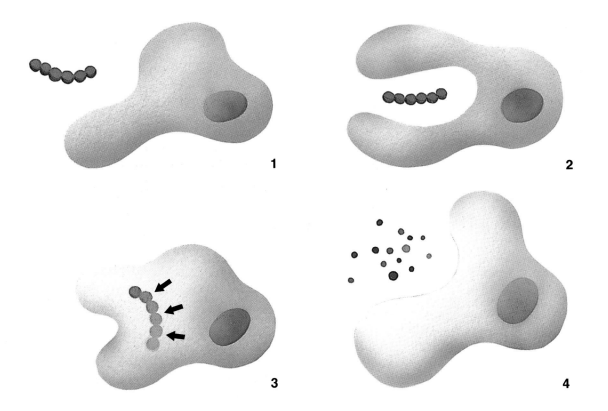

1

2

3

4

Arteries in trouble

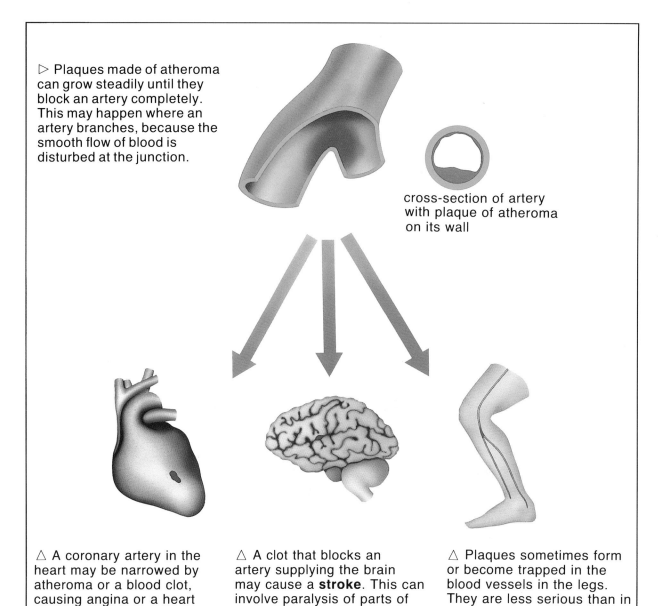

▷ Plaques made of atheroma can grow steadily until they block an artery completely. This may happen where an artery branches, because the smooth flow of blood is disturbed at the junction.

cross-section of artery with plaque of atheroma on its wall

△ A coronary artery in the heart may be narrowed by atheroma or a blood clot, causing angina or a heart attack (page 18) as the blood supply to the heart muscle is restricted.

△ A clot that blocks an artery supplying the brain may cause a **stroke**. This can involve paralysis of parts of the body and problems with speech.

△ Plaques sometimes form or become trapped in the blood vessels in the legs. They are less serious than in the heart or brain, but they can cause pain in the legs, especially when walking.

A continuous blood supply is vital in order for every body part to receive the oxygen and nutrients it needs. If an artery becomes blocked or diseased, the part of the body that relies on it may lose its blood supply – and if this happens it may die.

Two of the main problems that arteries can have are known as arteriosclerosis and atherosclerosis.

In arteriosclerosis, the arterial wall becomes more rigid and less elastic, so it cannot bulge to accommodate the surge of blood produced by each heartbeat. This is thought to be part of the normal ageing process.

Atherosclerosis involves the build-up of fatty lumps of material inside the artery, stuck to its wall. These narrow the space through which blood flows. The lumps are called plaques, and they are made of a fatty material known as atheroma. If a lump grows large enough, it may block the artery and prevent blood flow.

But there is a danger even if atheroma does not completely block an artery. As blood passes over the plaque, its smooth flow is disturbed, and it becomes more likely to clot. This clot, added to the plaque, may well block off the artery. Or the clot may break away and be carried along in the bloodstream until it reaches another, narrower blood vessel where it gets stuck and stops the blood flow. A blood clot that stays stuck where it forms is called a thrombus. A clot that breaks away and floats through the circulatory system is an embolus.

Disease of the arteries is linked to various aspects of health and lifestyle. It is made more likely by smoking cigarettes, having high blood pressure, eating too much fat in food (especially fats from animal sources), having high levels of **cholesterol** in the blood, being overweight and not getting enough exercise.

Heart attacks

Narrowing or blockage of the coronary arteries, which supply the heart's own muscle with blood, is a major cause of illness and death by heart attack in many countries. The problems usually appear in adult life, but some of their foundations are laid in childhood. Following these guidelines should reduce the risk of a heart attack in future years:

- Do not smoke.
- Do not become overweight.
- Do not eat too much fat, especially from animal sources such as dairy products and red meats.
- Get regular physical exercise.
- For adults, have your blood pressure checked regularly, and take measures to reduce it if it is too high.
- Women on the "pill" (oral contraceptive) should check with the doctor regularly.

Treatment of heart disease

Many different illnesses affect the heart, blood vessels and blood. Modern medical drugs and surgery can help to treat some of them, but there is no substitute for keeping your own heart and circulation healthy and active. Good habits learned in childhood, such as eating the right kind of food, getting plenty of exercise and not starting to smoke, will help to keep your heart and blood vessels in good condition for many years.

Some heart disorders are present at birth. In most cases, the complex "plumbing" of the heart and circulation has not developed correctly. There

Congenital heart disorders

- Symptoms of congenital heart disorders range from slight shortage of breath to life-threatening illness.
- In the UK, about 1 baby in 125 has such a heart disorder at birth.
- More than three-quarters of babies who need treatment in their first year will recover well and lead normal lives.

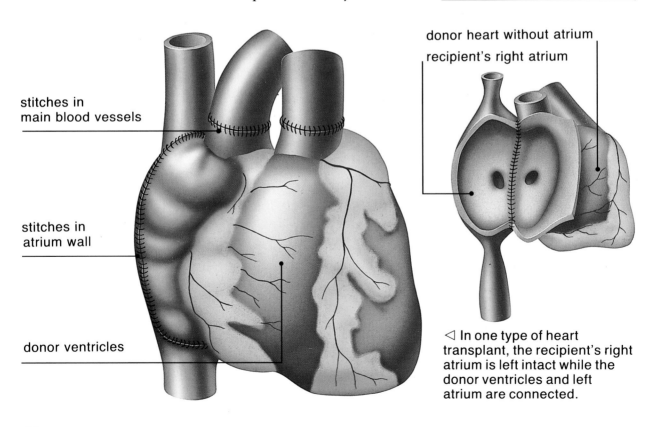

stitches in main blood vessels

stitches in atrium wall

donor ventricles

donor heart without atrium

recipient's right atrium

◁ In one type of heart transplant, the recipient's right atrium is left intact while the donor ventricles and left atrium are connected.

may be a "hole" between two heart chambers, or the vessels may be connected the wrong way round, so that blood does not flow properly around the body. The problem may be corrected immediately, by an operation on the newborn baby, but if the disorder is not too serious the doctors may wait for a few months, or even years, until the child is bigger and the operation is less risky.

Sometimes the heart's beating becomes unco-ordinated (arrhythmia), or it may pump too fast (tachycardia) or too slow (bradycardia) for the body's activities at the time. Some of these heart rhythm disorders can be treated by drugs that speed up or slow down the heart rate. For other rhythm problems, an artificial pacemaker is needed to take over from the heart's own faulty pacemaker (page 14).

Heart valves sometimes become damaged by disease, preventing proper blood circulation. This is termed valvular heart disease. In some cases the problem can be treated by replacing the damaged valve with an artificial implant made of plastic or metal. These materials are usually accepted by the body. They do not cause the problems of rejection that often arise when a living part from another person is used, as in a heart or kidney transplant.

If the heart pumps weakly, its muscular wall may be diseased. This is called cardiomyopathy. Sometimes it can be treated by drugs. In rare cases a heart transplant is required.

Nowadays, doctors can learn a lot about the heart without opening up the chest to look at it. Special X-rays, CAT scans, the "sound pictures" of echocardiography and the "electrical profiles" of ECGs all help to identify the trouble without the need for major surgery.

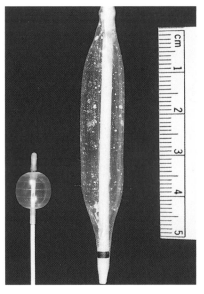

△ Tiny balloons are used in the modern technique of coronary angioplasty. Deflated, the balloon is threaded on the end of a long tube (catheter), through the skin and along a main blood vessel to the heart, and then into the coronary artery. Once in position, the balloon is inflated to move any blockage or widen a narrowed portion of the artery.

Lymph and lymph ducts

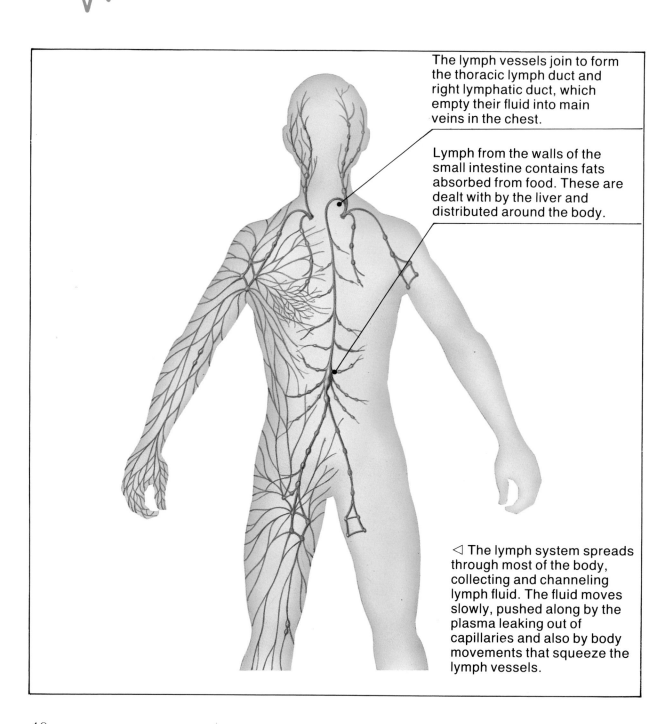

The lymph vessels join to form the thoracic lymph duct and right lymphatic duct, which empty their fluid into main veins in the chest.

Lymph from the walls of the small intestine contains fats absorbed from food. These are dealt with by the liver and distributed around the body.

◁ The lymph system spreads through most of the body, collecting and channeling lymph fluid. The fluid moves slowly, pushed along by the plasma leaking out of capillaries and also by body movements that squeeze the lymph vessels.

Capillaries are "leaky." Plasma passes between and through the cells in their walls, into the tissues beyond. The plasma carries with it many dissolved substances, including oxygen, nutrients and proteins such as antibodies.

The plasma that "leaks" into the tissues is called **lymph**. Eventually it is collected by the network of small tubes and ducts that form the lymph system. The ducts join together into larger lymph vessels, in the same way that capillaries come together to make veins. The vessels have one-way valves, like those in the larger veins.

The clear lymph fluid that flows through the system contains nutrients, white cells, proteins and other chemicals. It helps to distribute food materials and other essential substances, and it is a vital part of the body's defenses against infection and disease (page 42).

△ The tonsils, in the throat, contain concentrations of lymphatic tissue. By examining the throat, a doctor can tell if someone has an infection.

Lymph nodes and spleen

The lymph nodes are bulbous enlargements of lymph vessels, located in various places around the body. They are sometimes called lymph "glands," although they are not true glands. There are concentrations of lymph nodes in the neck, armpits and groin. When the body is invaded by germs, the white cells in the nodes multiply as part of the body's defense system (page 34). The lymph nodes swell to many times their usual size and become

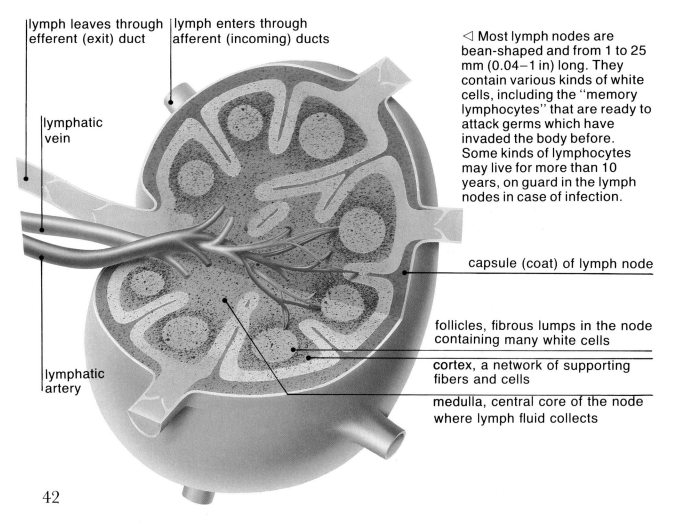

lymph leaves through efferent (exit) duct

lymph enters through afferent (incoming) ducts

lymphatic vein

lymphatic artery

◁ Most lymph nodes are bean-shaped and from 1 to 25 mm (0.04–1 in) long. They contain various kinds of white cells, including the "memory lymphocytes" that are ready to attack germs which have invaded the body before. Some kinds of lymphocytes may live for more than 10 years, on guard in the lymph nodes in case of infection.

capsule (coat) of lymph node

follicles, fibrous lumps in the node containing many white cells

cortex, a network of supporting fibers and cells

medulla, central core of the node where lymph fluid collects

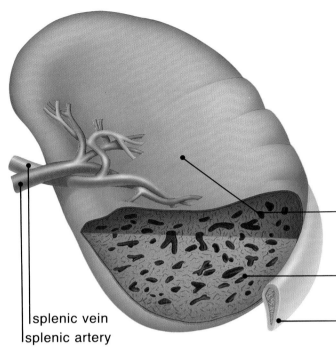

◁ The spleen is dark purple in color, spongy and grainy in texture, and has a large blood supply. It contains many phagocytes, white cells of the type that consume unwanted particles. They "eat" germs, old red cells and platelets, and they also dismantle small blood clots, helping to cleanse the blood.

capsule covering and protecting spleen

pulpy center of spleen contains many white cells

lower left rib

splenic vein
splenic artery

noticeable as tender bulges under the skin. These are the "swollen glands" that appear when the body is fighting an infection.

There are also patches of lymph-like tissue, called **lymphoid** tissue, in places such as the adenoids (at the back of the nasal cavity), the tonsils (in the throat), and the appendix and large intestine. They are thought to function like lymph nodes, filtering and cleaning the blood.

The spleen is another organ involved in the lymph system. It is kidney-shaped and about 12 centimeters (4.73 in) long, located in the upper left part of the abdomen, behind the stomach and at the level of the lower ribs. It contains many lymphocytes that make antibodies and release them into the bloodstream. It also breaks down old, worn-out red cells and platelets and recycles some of their contents to the bone marrow, liver and other organs. In early life the spleen makes red and white cells, but it is not essential in adults, so it can be removed if it becomes badly diseased.

The lymph system and AIDS

One of the first signs of the viral infection known as AIDS may be its effects on the lymph system.

● After entering the body, the AIDS virus (HIV, or Human Immuno-deficiency Virus) can lie dormant for a few years, with no ill effects.

● When the virus begins to multiply, the white cells become more numerous and try to fight back.

● This causes swelling of the lymph nodes, called lymphadenopathy.

● The virus gradually disables the white cells, so the body's immune defence system becomes damaged, or "deficient."

● AIDS stands for "Acquired Immune Deficiency Syndrome."

The artificial heart

In 1952, an American surgeon operated to implant the first artificial heart valve into a patient, to help her diseased aortic valve. The valve was a small metal ball inside a plastic tube. Its regular "tap-tap-tap," with each heartbeat, could be heard across the room. Since then, the designs for artificial heart valves, and for other "spare parts" for the heart and blood vessels, have improved enormously (page 38). They are now very reliable, and many thousands of patients receive them each year.

There have been attempts to make an entire artificial heart. One model is the Jarvik-7, named after its designer, Robert Jarvik. It consists of an aluminum base, two plastic chambers as the "ventricles," and four mechanical valves. It is powered by bursts of compressed air which travel from an air pump outside the body, along tubes that pass through the chest wall.

Two patients have received Jarvik-7 artificial hearts, in 1982 and 1984. The first lived for almost three months. The artificial heart itself performed well, but there were many other difficulties. Also, the patients had to stay near their pumps at all times, "tied" by the air lines.

Modern medicine can help the heart in many ways – from operations to repair holes and valves, to bypassing blocked coronary arteries, and implanting artificial devices such as pacemakers and valves. But there is no substitute for keeping your own heart fit and healthy, then it will hopefully beat efficiently for many years to come.

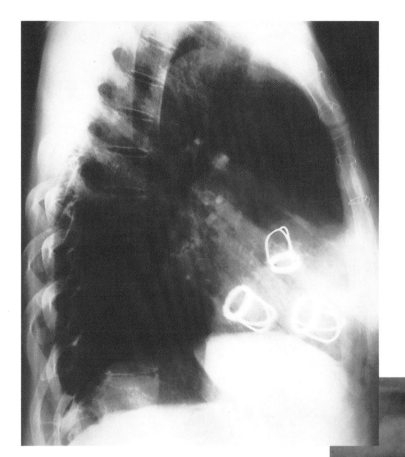

◁ Three Starr-Edwards "ball-and-cage" heart valves have been inserted into this patient's heart. The dense metal of the cages shows up clearly on an X-ray picture. The plastic balls they hold are only just visible as "shadows," since they are less dense, like body tissues. The ribs and backbone are also shown.

▷ The entrances and exits to the Jarvik 7 artificial heart, each guarded by a swinging-disk metal valve. The two chambers held in the hand are the heart's ventricles (there are no separate atria).

Glossary

Angina: severe pain in the chest, caused when arteries supplying blood to the heart muscle become narrowed and the heart is starved of oxygen.

Antibody: chemical substance produced by white blood cells, which immobilizes disease-producing organisms so they can be destroyed.

Antigen: substance on a germ or other foreign particle that provokes white blood cells to make antibodies.

Aorta: largest artery in the body, carrying blood pumped from the left ventricle.

Arteriole: narrow artery, which can become wider or narrower as required, to regulate the blood flow.

Arteries: vessels carrying blood *away* from the heart. Have thick, muscular walls to withstand the pressure.

Atrium: chamber in the upper part of the heart which receives blood from the body or lungs. There are two atria in the heart. Also called the auricle.

Blood: liquid containing chemicals and special cells, pumped around the body by the heart.

Blood group: type of blood, according to the agglutinogens (antigens) carried by red blood cells and agglutinins

(antibodies) in plasma. Includes the ABO system and Rhesus system.

Capillaries: the smallest blood vessels, carrying blood between arteries and veins. Capillary walls are very thin, to allow dissolved materials to pass through.

Carbon dioxide: (CO_2) colorless gas produced as a waste product by the body. Carried dissolved in the blood, to be removed by the lungs.

Cardiac muscle: special type of muscle in the walls of the heart. Its contractions cause the heart to pump.

Cholesterol: yellowish, fatty substance present in the blood. It may be deposited on the walls of arteries, where it restricts blood flow.

Circulatory system: passage of blood around and around the body.

Clot: (or thrombus) forms to prevent blood leaking from a damaged vessel. Clots are produced by chemical reaction between blood factors and platelets. They may sometimes form within an undamaged vessel, and if they break free in the bloodstream, cause blockages elsewhere in the circulation.

Deoxyhemoglobin: form

of hemoglobin which is low in oxygen. It is present in red blood cells when the blood returns to the heart from the body, having given up most of its oxygen to the tissues.

Electrocardiogram: (ECG) tracing of electrical impulses produced by the heart as it beats. An ECG can show up certain types of heart disease.

Erythrocyte: red blood cell.

Fibrin: yellow fibers produced by platelets from substances dissolved in the blood. Produces a clot to block a wound.

Hemoglobin: red substance containing iron, found in red blood cells. It combines easily with oxygen, which it carries around the body in the blood.

Heart: muscular pump which propels blood around the body, through the system of arteries, capillaries and veins.

Hormones: chemical messengers, carried in the blood.

Hypertension: high blood pressure, which can damage the heart, brain and kidneys if not treated.

Immune: when the body can resist invasion by the germs for a certain disease, having been infected by them previously and developed resistance.

Leucocyte: white blood cell.

Lymph: liquid from which red blood cells have been filtered, which collects in a special system before passing back into the blood. Important in fighting infection.

Lymph node: swelling in the lymph system, where bacteria and other debris are filtered from the lymph.

Lymphocytes: white blood cells that make antibodies in response to an infection

Lymphoid tissue: patches of tissue in the tonsils, adenoids, appendix and parts of the bowel, which filter bacteria from the lymph.

Oxygen: colorless gas that is needed by all living cells in the body. It is extracted from the air in the lungs, and carried about the body by hemoglobin in red blood cells.

Oxyhemoglobin: form of hemoglobin which is rich in oxygen. It is present in red blood cells when bright-red blood leaves the lungs after picking up oxygen from the air inside them.

Pacemaker: area in the right atrium which produces electrical impulses that cause the heart to beat regularly. If the natural pacemaker fails, an electronic one can be fitted surgically.

Pericardium: thin bag surrounding the heart. It contains liquid which lubricates the outside of the heart muscle as it pumps.

Plasma: clear liquid in which red and white blood cells are suspended. Plasma contains many food materials needed by the body, as well as dissolved wastes.

Platelets: (or thrombocytes) small pieces of cell, floating in the blood, which take part in the production of a blood clot to help close a wound.

Protein: chemical used to build and repair cells in the body.

Rhesus system: a system of blood grouping, in which an antigen called the Rhesus (Rh) factor is either present or not present on a person's red blood cells.

Septum: strong wall dividing left and right sides of the heart. A "hole in the heart" is a gap in the septum, allowing oxygenated blood to mix with deoxygenated blood. It can be corrected with surgery.

Sphygmomanometer: instrument used to measure blood pressure. An inflatable sleeve is fixed tightly around the upper arm, and pressure is measured on an instrument connected to the sleeve by a tube.

Spleen: spongy organ that forms part of the lymph system. It helps the body to fight infection. In babies, the spleen also produces red and white blood cells.

Stroke: results from the blockage or bursting of a blood vessel in the brain. Damage may be slight or very serious, depending on the part of the brain it affects.

Thrombocyte: platelet.

Thrombus: see **clot**.

Transfusion: the giving of blood from one person to another. It is necessary to establish the blood group of each person before this can be done safely.

Varicose veins: swollen, painful veins, caused by failure of the one-way valves that should prevent blood in the veins from flowing backward down the legs.

Veins: thin-walled blood vessels that return blood to the heart.

Venae cavae: superior and inferior venae cavae are the largest veins in the body, draining blood directly into the heart.

Ventricle: muscular chamber in the heart which pumps blood to the lungs (right ventricle) or around the body (left ventricle).

Index